The Best Sangria Cookbook

40 Drinks and Desserts Honoring Sangria

BY: Valeria Ray

License Notes

Copyright © 2019 Valeria Ray All Rights Reserved

All rights to the content of this book are reserved by the Author without exception unless permission is given stating otherwise.

The Author have no claims as to the authenticity of the content and the Reader bears all responsibility and risk when following the content. The Author is not liable for any reparations, damages, accidents, injuries or other incidents occurring from the Reader following all or part of this publication.

A Special Reward for Purchasing My Book!

Thank you, cherished reader, for purchasing my book and taking the time to read it. As a special reward for your decision, I would like to offer a gift of free and discounted books directly to your inbox. All you need to do is fill in the box below with your email address and name to start getting amazing offers in the comfort of your own home. You will never miss an offer because a reminder will be sent to you. Never miss a deal and get great deals without having to leave the house! Subscribe now and start saving!

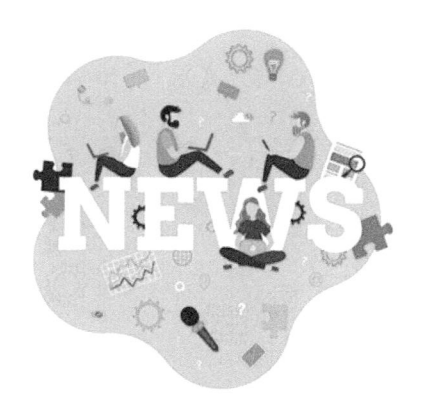

https://valeria-ray.gr8.com

Contents

Homemade Sangria Recipes 7

Chapter I - Sangria Drinks 8

    (1) White Wine, Elderflower and Ginger Sangria 9

    (2) Limoncello Sangria 11

    (3) Frosty Berry Licorice Sangria 13

    (4) Lavender Sangria 16

    (5) Basil Raspberry Rose Sangria 19

    (6) Tropical Sangria 22

    (7) Black Sangria 24

    (8) Thanksgiving Sangria 26

    (9) Bubblegum Sangria 28

    (10) Strawberry Shortcake Sangria 30

    (11) Caramel Apple Sangria 32

    (12) Rosé & Strawberry Sangria 34

(13) Chocolate Sangria 36

(14) Plum Sangria 38

(15) Christmas Cider Sangria 40

(16) Peach Sangria 42

(17) Coffee Brew Sangria 45

(18) Mystical Unicorn Sangria 47

(19) Greek Island Sangria 50

(20) Mojito Sangria 53

(21) Italian Sangria 55

(22) Mimosa Sangria 58

(23) Jasmine Iced Tea Sangria 60

(24) Mexican Sangria 62

(25) Lambrusco Sangria 64

Chapter II - Sangria Desserts and Sweet Treats 67

(26) Very Berry Sangria Sorbet 68

(27) Berrylicious Sangria Crumble 70

(28) Silky Sangria Panna Cotta 73

(29) Vanilla and Sangria Cake 77

(30) Drunken Truffles 80

(31) Summer Fruit Sangria Cobbler.................................... 82

(32) Fluffy Sangria Mousse 86

(33) Strawberry Sangria Jam... 90

(34) Fruity Sangria Salad with Ricotta Cream 93

(35) Spiked Sangria Bite-Sized Brownie............................. 96

(36) Over-21s Sangria Popsicles 99

(37) Spanish Sangria Poke Cake 101

(38) Raspberry-Peach White Sangria Trifle....................... 104

(39) Slim Sangria Jelly... 106

(40) Sangria Cupcakes 108

About the Author.. 112

Author's Afterthoughts... 114

Homemade Sangria Recipes

MMMMMMMMMMMMMMMMMMMMMMMMMMMMMMM

Chapter I - Sangria Drinks

(1) White Wine, Elderflower and Ginger Sangria

Floral, fragrant elderflower cordial combines with warm ginger and white wine to deliver sparkling sangria.

Yield: 6-8

Preparation Time: 5mins

List of Ingredients:

- 1 (750ml) bottle white wine
- ¾ cup ginger wine
- 1⅓ ounces elderflower cordial
- 1¼ cups sparkling bottled water
- 2 peaches (pitted, sliced)
- 2 limes (seeded, sliced)

Methods:

1. Add the white wine, ginger wine, elderflower cordial, and sparkling water to a jug.

2. Top with the peaches and limes, stir and serve.

(2) Limoncello Sangria

An Italian-inspired sangria made with limoncello and Pinot Grigio is an inexpensive party drink that your guests are sure to love.

Yield: 10

Preparation Time: 1hour

List of Ingredients:

- ½ cup granulated sugar
- ¼ cup water
- 1 cup limoncello
- 2 (750ml) bottles of Pinot Grigio
- 2-3 cups fruit of choice (chopped)
- 2 cups club soda

MMMMMMMMMMMMMMMMMMMMMMMMMMMMMMMM

Methods:

1. In a pan, combine the sugar with the water and over moderate-low heat, simmer until the sugar is entirely dissolved.

2. Transfer the syrup to a pitcher and stir in the limoncello, Pinot Grigio, and fruit of choice.

3. Transfer to the fridge to chill.

4. Just before serving, pour in the club soda.

(3) Frosty Berry Licorice Sangria

Sharp berries go hand in hand with the complex flavors of licorice, and this sangria not only looks good but also it tastes good too!

Yield: 2

Preparation Time: 20mins

List of Ingredients:

Ice cubes:

- ¼ cup blueberries
- ¼ cup blackberries

Berry Syrup:

- ¼ cup blueberries
- ¼ cup blackberries
- ½ cup sugar
- ½ cup water
- 6-8 mint leaves

Sangria:

- 6 ounces berry syrup
- 1½ cups Pinot Grigio
- 2 teaspoons freshly squeezed lime juice
- 2 teaspoons licorice liqueur
- Berries (to garnish)
- Mint leaves (to garnish)

MMMMMMMMMMMMMMMMMMMMMMMMMMMMMM

Methods:

1. Divide the blueberries and blackberries between 9-12 ice cube compartments. Fill each cube with water and freeze.

2. To make the syrup: Bring the blueberries and blackberries along with the sugar, and water to a boil, while continually whisking to dissolve the sugar entirely.

3. Remove from the heat and add the mint leaves. Mash the berries with the mint in the syrup and cool for half an hour to allow the flavors to fuse.

4. Strain the syrup through a fine nylon mesh sieve and discard the resulting mash.

5. Gently stir the syrup with the wine, lime juice, and licorice liqueur.

6. Evenly divided the berry-filled ice cubes between 2 wine goblets and pour in the sangria.

7. Garnish with berries and mint.

(4) Lavender Sangria

Invite the fragrance and flavor of lavender into your kitchen. Lavender-infused sangria is a joy to the senses.

Yield: 4-6

Preparation Time: 30mins

List of Ingredients:

Lavender Simple Syrup:

- ½ cup sugar
- ½ cup water
- 2 teaspoons dried culinary lavender
- 2 sprigs fresh lavender

Sangria:

- 1 pint of strawberries (hulled, sliced)
- 1 (10 ounce) bag frozen peaches
- 1 (750ml) bottle Pinot Grigio
- ½ cup brandy
- ½ cup orange liqueur
- 2 cups club soda

MMMMMMMMMMMMMMMMMMMMMMMMMMMMMMMM

Methods:

1. First, make the syrup: Over moderate to low heat, add the sugar, water and culinary lavender to a pan.

2. Whisk the mixture until the sugar is entirely dissolved, and bring to simmer.

3. Cook for 60 seconds before removing from the heat and set the pan aside to allow the syrup to completely cool.

4. When cooled, strain the syrup through a fine nylon mesh sieve. Discard the lavender.

5. Store the syrup in the fridge until needed.

6. For the sangria: Add the strawberries and peaches to a large pitcher.

7. Pour in the wine, followed by the brandy, orange liqueur and 1/3 cup of lavender syrup. Taste and add additional syrup if needed.

8. Add the club soda and stir to combine.

9. Serve over ice.

(5) Basil Raspberry Rose Sangria

Bursting with berry flavor and combined with wine, vodka, and raspberry liqueur, this sangria will certainly get the party started.

Yield: 8

Preparation Time: 2hours 15mins

List of Ingredients:

- 2 cups raspberries (divided)
- ½ cup fresh basil leaves (chopped)
- ¼ cup superfine sugar
- ¼ cup freshly squeezed lime juice
- 1 (750 ml) bottle rose wine
- 1 cup vodka
- ¼ cup raspberry liqueur
- 3 cups raspberry seltzer
- 1 lime (seeded, thinly sliced)
- Ice

Methods:

1. In a large pitcher or jug, combine 1 cup of raspberries, chopped basil leaves, sugar, and fresh lime juice and with a wooden spoon muddle until incorporated.

2. Pour in the rose wine along with the vodka and liqueur. Transfer to the fridge for 2 hours; this will allow the flavors to intensify.

3. Add the raspberry seltzer along with the lime slices and remaining raspberries.

4. Serve the sangria over ice.

(6) Tropical Sangria

Sangria goes tropical with white rum, pineapple juice and a selection of fresh fruit.

Yield: 4

Preparation Time: 10mins

List of Ingredients:

- 1 (750ml) bottle Moscato white wine
- 1 cup white rum
- 6 ounces pineapple juice
- ½ cup freshly squeezed orange juice
- Fresh pineapple, oranges, strawberries, mango (chopped)

MMMMMMMMMMMMMMMMMMMMMMMMMMMMMMMMM

Methods:

1. Combine the white wine, white rum, pineapple juice, orange juice, and fresh fruit in a large pitcher and transfer to the fridge to chill.

2. Serve and enjoy.

(7) Black Sangria

Sass up that sangria with a dark juice and black fruits.

Yield: 4

Preparation Time: 8hours 15mins

List of Ingredients:

- 1 (750-ml) bottle Malbec or cabernet sauvignon
- ½ cup blueberry juice
- ¼ cup brandy
- ¼ cup pure maple syrup
- 1 cup blackberries
- 2 black plums (pitted, chopped into wedges)
- 1 cup black grapes (halved)

MMMMMMMMMMMMMMMMMMMMMMMMMMMMMMMMMM

Methods:

1. In a large jug or pitcher, add the wine, blueberry juice, brandy, maple syrup (to sweeten), blackberries, plum, and grapes. Stir to combine.

2. Set the sangria aside to sit, overnight.

3. Serve over ice and add some of the alcohol-soaked fruits to each of the ice-filled glasses.

(8) Thanksgiving Sangria

This fruity libation is not only perfect for a Thanksgiving celebration but also for any time you get your family and friends in party mood.

Yield: 6-8

Preparation Time: 3hours 10mins

List of Ingredients:

- 2 apples (cored, diced)
- 1 orange (seeded, sliced)
- Arils of 1 pomegranate
- Superfine sugar (to taste)
- 1 (750ml) bottle Spanish red wine
- ¼ cup brandy
- ¼ cup triple sec
- 1 (750ml) bottle sweet Champagne

MMMMMMMMMMMMMMMMMMMMMMMMMMMMMMMMM

Methods:

1. In a large jug or pitcher, add the apples, oranges, pomegranate arils, sugar (to taste), red wine, brandy and triple sec. Stir to combine, transfer to the fridge for 2-3 hours to chill.

2. When you are ready to serve, pour in the Champagne, gently stir and serve.

(9) Bubblegum Sangria

Bring out your inner kid with this gum ball-inspired boozy beverage.

Yield: 8

Preparation Time: 12hours 10mins

List of Ingredients:

- ¼ cup gumballs
- 1 cup vodka
- 1 (750ml) bottle red wine
- 1 cup strawberry or watermelon-flavor sparkling water
- 1 peach (pitted, sliced)
- 1 orange (seeded, sliced)
- ½ cup raspberries

MMMMMMMMMMMMMMMMMMMMMMMMMMMMMMMM

Methods:

1. Add the gumballs to a jar.

2. Pour the vodka over the gumballs and cover. Set aside to sit for 12 hours.

3. In a jug or pitcher, combine the vodka-soaked gumballs with the red wine, sparkling water, peaches, oranges, and raspberries.

4. Serve over ice.

(10) Strawberry Shortcake Sangria

This strawberry shortcake sangria tastes just as good as its cookie counterpart. Garnish with a fresh strawberry for a berrylicious pretty in pink beverage.

Yield: 1

Preparation Time: 6mins

List of Ingredients:

- Strawberries (hulled, sliced)
- 2 ounces whipped cream vodka
- 2 (750ml) bottles pink Moscato
- Splash of club soda
- 1 ounce strawberry liqueur
- Graham cracker crumbs (to rim)
- Small strawberry (to garnish)

MMMMMMMMMMMMMMMMMMMMMMMMMMMMMMMMM

Methods:

1. Add the slices of strawberries to a large jug.

2. Pour the vodka, Moscato, club soda and strawberry liqueur over the top of the strawberries and stir to combine.

3. Rime the glass with cracker crumbs and garnish with a strawberry.

(11) Caramel Apple Sangria

Apple and caramel feature in so many dessert recipes as the perfect pairing so it makes perfect sense that both should feature in this winter sangria.

Yield: 6-8

Preparation Time: 8hours 10mins

List of Ingredients:

- 2 firm, ripe apples (cored, sliced)
- 1 (750ml) bottle Chardonnay
- 1 (750ml) bottle Riesling
- 2 cups unfiltered apple cider
- 6 ounces caramel flavored vodka

Methods:

1. Add the apples to a large jug or pitcher.

2. Pour in the Chardonnay along with the Riesling, apple cider and flavored vodka. Stir well to combine.

3. Transfer to the fridge, overnight to chill.

4. Serve the sangria over ice.

(12) Rosé & Strawberry Sangria

Get out the party hats, invite some friends around and enjoy this sparkling sangria.

Yield: 4-6

Preparation Time: 5mins

List of Ingredients:

- 3 cups rose wine
- ¼ cup orange liqueur
- Freshly squeezed juice of 1 orange
- 1 tablespoon caster sugar
- 1 ¼ cups sparkling bottled water
- Strawberries (hulled, sliced)
- Mint (chopped, to serve)

MMMMMMMMMMMMMMMMMMMMMMMMMMMMMMMMMM

Methods:

1. Pour the rose into a jug.

2. Add the liqueur along with the fresh orange juice, caster sugar, and sparkling water.

3. Top with the strawberries, garnish with mint.

4. Stir and serve.

(13) Chocolate Sangria

Chocolate lovers will go crazy for this decadent and indulgent sangria.

Yield: 2-4

Preparation Time: 6mins

List of Ingredients:

- 1 (750ml) chocolate wine
- ½ cup hazelnut liqueur
- ½ cup vodka
- 1-2 cups fresh strawberries (hulled, sliced)

Methods:

1. Combine the chocolate wine, hazelnut liqueur, vodka and strawberries to a large jug.

2. Stir to combine and serve.

(14) Plum Sangria

Tart plum tastes particularly good with almond flavor amaretto and sweet fruit.

Yield: 2-4

Preparation Time: 10mins

List of Ingredients:

- 1 (750ml) bottle Sauvignon Blanc
- ½ cup amaretto
- ½ (12 ounce) can white soda
- 1 plum (pitted, finely sliced)
- ½ nectarine (seeded, thinly sliced)
- ½ cup frozen sweet cherries

MMMMMMMMMMMMMMMMMMMMMMMMMMMMMMMMMM

Methods:

1. In a pitcher, combine the wine with the amaretto, white soda, plum, nectarine, and frozen cherries.

2. Transfer to the fridge until you are ready to serve.

(15) Christmas Cider Sangria

This Christmas sangria will be a huge hit at your next festive party or get together. Everyone will love sharing this fruity, spicy blend.

Yield: 6

Preparation Time: 1hour 15mins

List of Ingredients:

- 4 cups red wine
- 2 cups apple cider
- ½ cup triple sec
- Juice of 1 fresh orange
- 2 apples (cored, sliced)
- 1 orange (seeded, sliced)
- ½ cup pomegranate arils
- 2 cinnamon sticks
- 2 tablespoons star anise

MMMMMMMMMMMMMMMMMMMMMMMMMMMMMMMMM

Methods:

1. In a punch bowl, combine the red wine with the apple cider, triple sec, and fresh orange juice.

2. Add the slices of apple along with the orange slices, pomegranate arils, cinnamon sticks, and star anise.

3. Set aside for a minimum of 60 minutes and a maximum of 9 hours.

4. Stir before serving, and serve chilled.

(16) Peach Sangria

Crisp, refreshing and peachy keen! What more could you ask for?

Yield: 8

Preparation Time: 8hours 10mins

List of Ingredients:

- 1 pound fresh yellow peaches (pitted, sliced)
- ¼ cup sugar
- ½ cup water
- ¾ cup peach schnapps
- 1 (750ml) bottle of white wine
- 1 quart ginger ale (chilled)

MMMMMMMMMMMMMMMMMMMMMMMMMMMMMMM

Methods:

1. Add the slices of peach to the bottom of a punch bowl or large pitcher.

2. In a pan, bring the sugar and water to boil and stir until the sugar is entirely dissolved.

3. Remove the pan from the heat and set the syrup aside to cool.

4. Pour the syrup along with the peach schnapps and white wine over the peaches and stir.

5. Transfer the punch bowl to the fridge, overnight.

6. When you are ready to serve, fill the pitcher with the ginger ale and stir.

7. Serve the sangria in wine glasses.

(17) Coffee Brew Sangria

Join in the latest craze, sangria made with black coffee, red wine, orange liqueur, and fruit. We guarantee you won't miss the cream and sugar!

Yield: 8

Preparation Time: 45mins

List of Ingredients:

- 32 ounces cold brew coffee
- 16 ounces red wine
- 8 ounces tequila
- 4 ounces orange liqueur
- 1 tablespoon simple syrup
- 1 orange (seeded, sliced)
- 1 lime (seeded, sliced)

Methods:

1. In a large pitcher combine the cold brew with the red wine, tequila, orange liqueur, and simple syrup, stir well to combine.

2. Add the orange and lime and transfer to the fridge for 60 minutes.

3. Pour into ice-filled glasses and serve.

(18) Mystical Unicorn Sangria

Go rogue and add a little fun to this colorful ice cream with a scoop of raspberry ice cream

Yield: 4-6

Preparation Time: 15mins

List of Ingredients:

- ½ cup fresh raspberries
- ½ cup fresh blueberries
- 3 tablespoons sugar
- ⅓ cup blue Curacao
- 1 (750 ml) bottle of sweet, sparkling wine
- 1 -2 cups clear soda
- 1 scoop of raspberry ice cream (for each serving)
- Gold sugar sprinkles

MMMMMMMMMMMMMMMMMMMMMMMMMMMMMMMM

Methods:

1. Add the berries along with the sugar to a large jug and with a wooden spoon, muddle.

2. Pour in the blue Curacao and once again muddle.

3. Add the sparkling wine and clear soda, and stir to combine.

4. Pour the sangria into the glasses and add a scoop of ice cream into each glass.

5. Garnish with gold sugar sprinkles.

6. Serve and feel the magic!

(19) Greek Island Sangria

Say Yammas! And raise a glass to National Sangria Day with this sensational sangria.

Yield: 10-15

Preparation Time: 25mins

List of Ingredients:

Syrup:

- 2 cups of water
- 1 cup sugar
- 2-3 strips of orange or lemon peel
- 1 cinnamon stick
- 4-5 whole cloves
- ½ cup Greek honey

Sangria:

- 1 (750ml) bottle red wine
- 1 ripe peach (pitted, sliced)
- 1 orange (seeded, sliced)
- 2 (12 ounces) cans ginger ale
- ½ cup Greek brandy

MMMMMMMMMMMMMMMMMMMMMMMMMMMMMMMM

Methods:

1. First, make the syrup by adding the water, sugar, orange peel, cinnamon, and cloves to a pot and bring to boil.

2. Reduce the heat to simmer and boil for an additional 6 minutes.

3. Remove from the heat, add the honey and set aside to cool. Remove the citrus peel, cinnamon stick, and cloves, and discard.

4. Pour in the wine along with the slices of peach, orange, ginger ale and brandy, stir to combine.

5. In increments, add 1 cup of the syrup until you achieve your desired level of sweetness.

6. Serve the sangria over ice.

(20) Mojito Sangria

A classic cocktail gets a makeover to deliver a sparkling sangria.

Yield: 6

Preparation Time: 10mins

List of Ingredients:

- 20 mint leaves
- ½ cup simple syrup
- ¼ cup freshly squeezed lime juice
- 1 cup white rum
- 1 (750ml) bottle sparkling wine (chilled)
- 3 fresh limes (seeded, cut into wedges)
- Club soda

MMMMMMMMMMMMMMMMMMMMMMMMMMMMMMMMM

Methods:

1. Muddle the mint with the syrup.

2. Add the lime juice, mint syrup, rum, sparkling wine and limes in a large jug.

3. Serve in tall glasses and top with club soda.

(21) Italian Sangria

Lots of orange and lemon flavors combine to give this rich and flavorful sangria a citrus kick.

Yield: 6-8

Preparation Time: 6hours 10mins

List of Ingredients:

- 1 large navel orange
- 1 (750ml) bottle of Chianti red wine
- 4 ounces limoncello
- 2 ounces orange bitters
- 2 ounces triple sec
- 1 ounce simple syrup
- Angostura bitters
- Orange wedges (seeded, to garnish)

MMMMMMMMMMMMMMMMMMMMMMMMMMMMMMMM

Methods:

1. Cut 2 slices from the middle of the center of the orange and muddle in the bottom of a large jug.

2. Juice the remainder of the orange and add to the jug along with the Chianti, limoncello, orange bitters, triple sec and simple syrup. Stir well to combine.

3. Chill the sangria in the fridge for 4-6 hours, to allow the flavors to blend.

4. Pour the sangria over ice and add 2 splashes of Angostura bitters to each of the glasses.

5. Garnish with an orange wedge.

(22) Mimosa Sangria

Sangria made with chilled Champagne makes the best brunch beverage ever!

Yield: 8-10

Preparation Time: 2hours 8mins

List of Ingredients:

- 3 cups orange juice
- ½ cup orange liqueur
- 1 navel orange (seeded, quartered, thinly sliced)
- 2 cups fresh strawberries (hulled, thinly sliced)
- 1 cup fresh pineapple (peeled, diced)
- 1 (750 ml) bottle Champagne (chilled)
- Ice

MMMMMMMMMMMMMMMMMMMMMMMMMMMMMMMM

Methods:

1. In a jug or large pitcher, combine the fresh orange juice with the orange liqueur, sliced orange, strawberries, and pineapple. Using a wooden spoon, muddle the fruit.

2. Transfer the jug to the fridge to chill for 2 hours.

3. When you are ready to serve, fill your serving glasses ¼ full of the orange-fruit mixture.

4. Slowly fill each glass to full with Champagne.

5. Add ice if needed and serve.

(23) Jasmine Iced Tea Sangria

Fruity and fragrant this jasmine tea sangria is the perfect long drink to serve over ice.

Yield: 6

Preparation Time: 10mins

List of Ingredients:

- 4 cups fresh brewed jasmine iced tea
- 2 cups white wine
- Honey (to taste)
- 1 cup nectarines (pitted, chopped)
- 1 cup strawberries (hulled, sliced)

MMMMMMMMMMMMMMMMMMMMMMMMMMMMMMMM

Methods:

1. In a pitcher, combine jasmine tea, white wine, and honey (to taste) and stir.

2. Transfer to the fridge, overnight.

3. When you are ready to serve, add the nectarines along with the strawberries and serve chilled.

(24) Mexican Sangria

Two favorite drinks combine in a large pitcher to make the perfect party drink.

Yield: 10-12

Preparation Time: 2hours 10mins

List of Ingredients:

- 1 (750ml) bottle of Chardonnay
- 1½ cups tequila
- 1 cup triple sec
- 1 cup fresh orange juice
- ½ cup fresh lime juice
- 1 medium orange (seeded, sliced)
- 2-3 stems of cilantro
- Sea salt (to rim)
- Crushed ice (to serve)

Methods:

1. In a large jug or pitcher combine the Chardonnay with the tequila, triple sec, orange juice, and lime juice.

2. Add the slices of orange along with the cilantro.

3. Transfer the sangria to the fridge and chill for 2 hours.

4. Rim the glasses with the sea salt.

5. Serve over crushed ice.

(25) Lambrusco Sangria

Lambrusco is sweet and sparkling and is perfect for sangria especially combined with spiced syrup, orange juice, and warm spices.

Yield: 8-10

Preparation Time: 50mins

List of Ingredients:

Spiced Syrup:

- 1½ cups water
- ½ cup sugar
- 8 cloves
- 10 cardamom pods (crushed)
- 2 cinnamon sticks

Sangria:

- 2 Fuji apples (cored, cut into ½" dice)
- 1 orange (peeled, seeded, cut into 1" pieces)
- ½ cup orange liqueur
- ½ cup freshly squeezed orange juice
- 2 (750 ml) bottles Italian Lambrusco
- 2 cups club soda

MMMMMMMMMMMMMMMMMMMMMMMMMMMMMMMMMM

Methods:

1. To make the syrup: In a small pan, combine the water with the sugar, cloves, cardamom, and cinnamon.

2. Over moderate heat, bring to simmer and cook for 2 minutes, to entirely dissolve the sugar.

3. Allow to completely cool before straining. Transfer to the fridge for up to 4-5 days and use as needed.

4. For the sangria: In a punch bowl, combine the apples with the oranges, liqueur, fresh orange juice, and ½ a cup of the prepared spiced syrup. Using a wooden spoon, stir to combine. Allow to rest for 20 minutes.

5. Pour in the Lambrusco along with the club soda and stir to incorporate.

6. Serve the sangria over ice.

Chapter II - Sangria Desserts and Sweet Treats

MMMMMMMMMMMMMMMMMMMMMMMMMMMMMMM

(26) Very Berry Sangria Sorbet

Sorbet is a refreshing and light dessert to have on hand in the freezer.

Yield: 6-8

Preparation Time: 8hours 5mins

List of Ingredients:

- ¾ cup sweet red wine
- 5 cups mixed frozen berries
- 2 tablespoons granulated sugar
- ½ teaspoons fresh lemon juice
- 2 tablespoons corn syrup

MMMMMMMMMMMMMMMMMMMMMMMMMMMMMMMM

Methods:

1. Add the wine, berries, sugar, lemon juice, and corn syrup to a blender and blitz until smooth.

2. Transfer the mixture to a freezer-safe resealable container and freeze overnight.

3. Allow to stand at room temperature for several minutes before serving.

(27) Berrylicious Sangria Crumble

Warm, juicy berries sit underneath a golden, crunchy crumble for a flavor and texture sensation.

Yield: 4-6

Preparation Time: 1hour

List of Ingredients:

Fruit:

- 12 ounces fresh strawberries (hulled, quartered)
- 12 ounces fresh raspberries
- 12 ounces fresh blueberries
- Juice and zest of 1 fresh lime
- 2 tablespoons flour
- 3 tablespoons granulated sugar
- ¼ teaspoons salt
- 3 tablespoons orange liqueur
- 3 tablespoons red wine

Crumble:

- 1⅓ cups brown sugar
- 1⅓ cups oats
- ½ cup flour
- ¼ teaspoons salt
- ½ teaspoons cinnamon
- 6 tablespoons butter (at room temperature)
- 1 teaspoon vanilla essence
- Vanilla ice cream (to serve)

MMMMMMMMMMMMMMMMMMMMMMMMMMMMMMMM

Methods:

1. Preheat the main oven to 375 degrees F.

2. Combine all of the fresh berries in a 13x9" tin. Pour over the lime juice and zest, gently toss to combine.

3. In a bowl, combine the flour, sugar, and salt. Scatter the mixture over the fruit and toss again. Set aside for 10 minutes. Pour over the orange liqueur and wine.

4. Next, prepare the crumble. Combine the sugar, oats, flour, salt, and cinnamon. Add the butter to the mixture and combine using clean fingers until crumbly. Add the vanilla essence.

5. Scatter the mixture over the fruit.

6. Place in the oven and bake for just over half an hour until golden.

7. Serve warm with vanilla ice cream.

(28) Silky Sangria Panna Cotta

Silky smooth Italian custard is infused with cinnamon, honey, red wine and topped with diced apple for a delicious boozy dessert.

Yield: 6

Preparation Time: 9hours 15mins

List of Ingredients:

- 2 medium oranges
- 7 tablespoons granulated sugar
- 3 cups dry red wine
- 1 cinnamon stick
- 2 teaspoons honey
- 1 cup whole milk
- 1 (0.25 ounce) sachet powdered gelatin
- 2 cups plain yogurt
- 1 green apple (cored, diced)

MMMMMMMMMMMMMMMMMMMMMMMMMMMMMMMM

Methods:

1. Carefully remove a 2-3" piece of zest from one of the oranges. Take the zest of the second orange. Next, peel each orange and separate the segments. Cover and chill.

2. Combine 5 tablespoons of the sugar with the wine, cinnamon stick, orange peel, and honey in a saucepan over moderately low heat. Bring to a simmer and cook for 40 minutes until thick and well reduced. Remove the cinnamon stick and orange peel. Take off the heat and allow to completely cool. Set aside ½ a cup of the liquid to serve.

3. In a clean saucepan combine the milk, with the remaining sugar and gelatine. Set aside for 5 minutes.

4. Place over moderate heat and gently cook for a few minutes while stirring until the sugar and gelatin dissolve. Allow to cool.

5. Add 1 cup of the reduced wine to the gelatin mixture along with the orange zest, and plain yogurt, stir to combine. Divide the mixture between 6 ramekins, cover, and chill overnight.

6. When ready to serve, combine the diced apple and orange segments.

7. Turn the panna cottas out of the ramekins and onto serving plates. Top each with fruit and drizzle with reserved wine syrup. Serve.

(29) Vanilla and Sangria Cake

Celebrate National Sangria Day with a slice of this frosted moist cake.

Yield: 8

Preparation Time: 1hour 15mins

List of Ingredients:

- Butter and flour (for tin)

Cake:

- 1 cup granulated sugar
- ½ cup + 6 tablespoons unsalted butter (at room temperature)
- Zest of ½ a medium orange
- 2 medium eggs
- 1 teaspoon vanilla essence
- 1 teaspoon baking powder
- 1½ cups all-purpose flour
- ¾ cup prepared red wine sangria
- Purple food gel

Frosting:

- 1 cup confectioner's sugar
- 4 tablespoons unsalted butter (at room temperature)
- 2½ tablespoons heavy cream
- Zest of ½ a medium orange
- Pinch salt

Methods:

1. Preheat the main oven to 350 degrees. Grease and flour an 8" cake tin.

2. Using an electric mixer, beat together the sugar, butter, and orange zest until fluffy.

3. Next, beat in the eggs one at a time and vanilla essence. Followed by the baking powder and flour. Mix until just incorporated.

4. Fold in the sangria then color with your desired level of purple food gel.

5. Transfer the batter to the cake tin and bake in the oven for 20 minutes. Remove, cover with foil, and cook for another 10 minutes. Allow to completely cool.

6. In the meantime, prepare the frosting. Beat together the confectioner's sugar, butter, heavy cream, orange zest, and salt until thick and fluffy. Use this mixture to frost the cooled cake.

7. Slice and serve.

(30) Drunken Truffles

With just three ingredients you can whip up a batch of decadently rich melt-in-the-mouth sangria truffles.

Yield: 16

Preparation Time: 5hours

List of Ingredients:

- 8 ounces milk chocolate candy bar
- 1 teaspoon brandy
- ¼ cup dry red wine
- 1 teaspoon orange liqueur
- Cocoa powder (for rolling)

MMMMMMMMMMMMMMMMMMMMMMMMMMMMMMMM

Methods:

1. Break the chocolate into small pieces and transfer to an 8" glass baking dish.

2. Melt using a microwave and stir until smooth.

3. Add the brandy, wine, and liqueur and stir to combine. Set out at room temperature for a few hours until solid.

4. Using a tablespoon, roll the mixture into 1" balls then coat each ball with cocoa powder. Transfer to a resealable container and chill until ready to serve. Allow to come to room temperature before enjoying.

(31) Summer Fruit Sangria Cobbler

Juicy black plums and jewel-toned cherries are the perfect partners to sweet and soft buttermilk cobbler.

Yield: 8

Preparation Time: 1hour 30mins

List of Ingredients:

Fruit Filling:

- 1 cup pitted cherries
- 1 pound ripe black plums (stoned, sliced)
- 1 apple (cored, diced)
- Juice and zest of 1 lemon
- Juice and zest of 1 orange
- 3 tablespoons granulated sugar
- 2 tablespoons cornstarch
- ½ cup sweet red wine

Cobbler Topping:

- 1¼ cup flour
- 5 tablespoons granulated sugar
- Pinch salt
- 1½ teaspoons baking powder
- 2 tablespoons melted butter
- 1 medium egg
- ½ cup buttermilk
- 1 teaspoon orange zest (grated)

MMMMMMMMMMMMMMMMMMMMMMMMMMMMMMMMMMM

Methods:

1. Preheat the main oven to 375 degrees F.

2. Arrange a 1½-quart baking dish on a baking tray. Set to one side.

3. First, prepare the fruit filling. In a large bowl, toss all of the fruit with the citrus zest and juice and sugar.

4. Whisk together the cornstarch and wine then pour over the fruit mixture. Gently toss to combine. Transfer the mixture to the baking dish.

5. Next, prepare the cobbler topping. Combine the flour, 4 tablespoons sugar, salt, and baking powder in a bowl. Make a well in the center.

6. In a jug, beat together the melted butter, egg, and buttermilk and mix into the dry ingredients a little at a time until incorporated.

7. Drop the batter in spoonfuls on top of the fruit.

8. Combine the orange zest with the remaining sugar and sprinkle over the dough.

9. Place in the oven and bake for approximately 40 minutes until golden.

10. Serve warm.

(32) Fluffy Sangria Mousse

This sangria-flavored mousse is super fluffy and light with bold fruity flavor.

Yield: 6

Preparation Time: 8hours 10mins

List of Ingredients:

- 4 gelatine sheets
- 5¼ ounces granulated sugar
- ⅓ cup + 1 tablespoon red port wine
- 1 cup dry red wine
- 2 tablespoons fresh lemon juice
- 1 teaspoon lemon peel (grated)
- Juice and zest of 2 oranges
- Yolks of 2 medium eggs
- 1⅔ cups heavy whipping cream
- 1 (0.3 ounce) sachet vanilla sugar

MMMMMMMMMMMMMMMMMMMMMMMMMMMMMMMMMMM

Methods:

1. Soak the sheets of gelatine in a bowl of water for 5 minutes.

2. Add 3½ ounces of the sugar to a saucepan along with the wines and bring to a boil. Cook for just over 10 minutes until thick and syrupy. Add the lemon juice and peel to the pan along with the soaked gelatin leaves. Stir until the gelatin dissolves. Take off the heat.

3. In a large bowl, beat together the orange juice, orange zest, egg yolk, and remaining sugar.

4. Using a double boiler, gently heat the egg yolk mixture while continually stirring. Fold the mixture into the wine mixture.

5. Using an electric whisk, whip up the mixture until creamy. Allow to cool completely.

6. In the meantime, whip the cream with the vanilla sugar until it can hold stiff peaks,

7. Fold the whipped cream into the wine mixture until incorporated.

8. Divide the mousse between serving glasses/bowls and chill overnight.

(33) Strawberry Sangria Jam

Bring a taste of summer to the breakfast table all-year round with this sweet jam.

Yield: 1 cup

Preparation Time: 24hours 10mins

List of Ingredients:

- 3 cups fresh strawberries (washed, hulled, chopped)
- ½ cup sugar
- 3 tablespoons red wine
- 1 tablespoon fresh orange juice
- 1 teaspoon fresh lemon juice
- 1 teaspoon orange liqueur

MMMMMMMMMMMMMMMMMMMMMMMMMMMMMMMMMM

Methods:

1. In a bowl, stir the strawberries together with the sugar, red wine, fresh orange juice, and fresh lemon juice. Using kitchen wrap, tightly cover the bowl and transfer to the fridge, overnight.

2. The following day, transfer the mixture to a food blender and on the pulse setting, process 2-3 times until you achieve a chunky puree-like consistency.

3. Scrape the puree into a shallow, wide pan over moderate-high heat and while frequently stirring, cook until the jam begins to thicken approximately 10 minutes.

4. Stir in the orange liqueur and spoon the jam into clean ½ pint jar.

5. Allow the jam to cool, in the jar, to room temperature. The jar needs to sit on a heat-proof surface.

6. Transfer the jar to the fridge.

7. The jam will keep for up to 28 days.

(34) Fruity Sangria Salad with Ricotta Cream

A light and delicious dessert is the perfect end to a heavy meal.

Yield: 4

Preparation Time: 30mins

List of Ingredients:

- ½ cup + 2 tablespoons granulated sugar
- 1½ cups dry red wine
- 2-3 strips of orange peel
- 2 cups mixed fresh berries
- ¼ teaspoons vanilla essence
- 1 tablespoon orange liqueur
- 8 ounces semi-skim ricotta cheese
- 1 teaspoon orange zest

MMMMMMMMMMMMMMMMMMMMMMMMMMMMMMMM

Methods:

1. Add the ½ cup sugar, red wine, and orange peel to a saucepan over moderately high heat until the sugar dissolves. Bring the mixture to a boil, and cook for 10-12 minutes until thick and syrups. Take off the heat, allow to cool, then discard the orange peel.

2. Add the berries to a bowl and pour over the prepared liquid.

3. Add the vanilla essence, orange liqueur, ricotta cheese, 1 teaspoon orange zest, 2 tablespoons sugar to a food processor and blitz until smooth.

4. Divide the berry mixture between 4 serving bowls and top with the ricotta mixture. Serve straight away.

(35) Spiked Sangria Bite-Sized Brownie

A rich fudge brownie spiked with a generous glug of red wine is topped with a sweet berry mixture and fluffy whip cream.

Yield: 18

Preparation Time: 1hour 15mins

List of Ingredients:

Brownie:

- 1 (19 ounce) box triple fudge brownie mix
- ¼ cup vegetable oil
- ⅓ cup dry red wine
- 2 tablespoons orange zest (freshly grated)
- 1 medium egg

Topping:

- 1 cup fresh strawberries (hulled, sliced)
- 1 cup fresh blackberries
- 1 cup fresh raspberries
- 3 tablespoons dry red wine
- 1 tablespoon granulated sugar
- Whipped cream (to serve)

MMMMMMMMMMMMMMMMMMMMMMMMMMMMMMMMM

Methods:

1. Preheat the main oven to 325 degrees F.

2. Line 2 (9-hole) muffin tins with cupcake liners.

3. In a large bowl, combine the brownie mix, vegetable oil, red wine, orange zest, and egg.

4. Divide the batter between the liners.

5. Place in the oven and cook for 25 minutes. Allow to completely cool.

6. In a bowl, toss together the fresh berries, red wine, and sugar. Chill for an hour.

7. Top each brownie bite with fruit and a dollop of whip cream. Serve.

(36) Over-21s Sangria Popsicles

Popsicles don't just have to be for kids, with red wine and summer fruit the grownups will love icy treats!

Yield: Dependent on size of popsicle mold

Preparation Time: 8hours 40mins

List of Ingredients:

- 1 cup granulated sugar
- 1 cup water
- 1 (0.4 ounce) sachet gelatine
- 2 cups fresh mixed fruit (chopped)
- 3 cups dry red wine

Methods:

1. Combine the sugar and water in a saucepan over moderate heat, bring to a boil and cook until the mixture reduces by half. Add the gelatine, stir to combine and take off the heat. Allow to cool.

2. Add half of the fruit to a blender and blitz until smooth.

3. In a jug, stir together the fruit puree, wine, and gelatine mixture.

4. Divide the remaining chopped fruit between holes in your chosen popsicle mold and pour over the popsicle mixture.

5. Freeze overnight.

(37) Spanish Sangria Poke Cake

Top this cocktail-inspired poke cake with a cloud of whip cream and serve with a glass of you guessed it; ice-cold sangria.

Yield: 12

Preparation Time: 5hours

List of Ingredients:

- 1 (18.25 ounce) package white cake mix (plus ingredients called for on box)
- 1 cup water
- ¼ cup brandy
- ¼ cup Riesling wine
- 3 ounces orange-flavored gelatin
- 1 pint heavy whipping cream
- 1 cup fresh raspberries
- 1 medium peach (stoned, sliced)

MMMMMMMMMMMMMMMMMMMMMMMMMMMMMMMM

Methods:

1. Preheat the main oven to 350 degrees F.

2. Prepare and bake the box mix using package instructions. Allow to completely cool.

3. When the cake has cooled, poke holes in it using a wooden skewer.

4. Next, bring the water to a boil in a saucepan. Take off the heat and stir in the brandy, wine, and gelatin. Pour the mixture over the cake. Chill for a few hours.

5. When ready to serve, whip up the cream until it can hold stiff peaks. Spoon on top of the cake and top with fresh fruit. Slice and serve.

(38) Raspberry-Peach White Sangria Trifle

A six-layered trifle is a childhood classic, but this raspberry-peach white sangria version is a fresh twist on an old-fashioned dessert.

Yield: 10-12

Preparation Time: 2hours 20mins

List of Ingredients:

- 5 ripe peaches (stoned, peeled, sliced)
- 1½ cups sweet white wine
- 2 cups heavy whipping cream
- 1 cup confectioner's sugar
- 15 ounces prepared pound cake (cubed)
- 6 ounces fresh raspberries

MMMMMMMMMMMMMMMMMMMMMMMMMMMMMMMMMM

Methods:

1. Add the peaches and white wine to a shallow dish and set aside to soak for a couple of hours.

2. Next, whip up the cream until it can hold semi-stiff peaks. Add 2 tablespoons of the peach soaking liquid along with the confectioner's sugar and continue to whip until stiff and fluffy.

3. To assemble the trifle, arrange half of the cubed cake in the base of a large serving dish. Top with half of the soaked peaches, half of the raspberries, and half of the whipped cream. Repeat these layers on more time.

4. Keep chilled until ready to serve.

(39) Slim Sangria Jelly

This deliciously wobbly sangria jelly is big on flavor but low on calories so you can satisfy your sweet tooth guilt-free.

Yield: 6

Preparation Time: 5hours 50mins

List of Ingredients:

- 1 (0.3 ounce) sachet sugar-free raspberry gelatin
- 1 (0.3 ounce) sachet sugar-free lemon gelatin
- 1½ cups boiling hot water
- 1 cup chilled water
- 1 cup dry white wine
- 11 ounces canned mandarin orange segments
- 1 cup fresh raspberries
- 1 cup diced green apple

MMMMMMMMMMMMMMMMMMMMMMMMMMMMMMMM

Methods:

1. Dissolve both gelatin powders in the boiling water in a large bowl. Set aside for 10 minutes then add the cold water and white wine, stir to combine. Chill for approximately 45 minutes until half set.

2. Add the fruit and gently stir to combine. Divide the mixture between serving glasses and chill for 4-5 hours until set.

(40) Sangria Cupcakes

These pretty pink sangria cupcakes are perfect for your next party or girly get-together.

Yield: 24

Preparation Time: 5hours 50mins

List of Ingredients:

Cake:

- 1 (16½ ounce) box lemon cake mix
- ¼ cup frozen orange juice concentrate (thawed)
- ¾ cup prepared red wine sangria
- 3 medium eggs
- ⅓ cup vegetable oil
- Red food gel

Filling:

- 1¼ cups prepared red wine sangria
- 2 tablespoons frozen orange juice concentrate (thawed)
- ¼ cup granulated sugar
- ¼ cup cornstarch
- ½ cup green apple (cored, finely diced)

Frosting:

- 1 cup prepared red wine sangria
- 1 cup butter (at room temperature)
- Pinch salt
- 4 cups powdered sugar
- 2 teaspoons frozen orange juice concentrate (thawed)

Methods:

1. Preheat the main oven to 350 degrees F and line two 12-hole muffin tins with cupcake liners.

2. First, prepare the cupcakes. Beat together the cake mix, orange concentrate, sangria, eggs, and vegetable oil until combined. Add your desired level of red food gel and stir well.

3. Divide the batter between the cupcake liners and bake in the oven for just under 20 minutes. Allow to completely cool.

4. In the meantime, prepare the filling. Combine the sangria, orange concentrate, sugar, and cornstarch in a saucepan over moderate heat continually stirring until thick and bubbling. Fold in the apple and transfer to a small bowl. Cover tightly with plastic wrap and chill.

5. Next, prepare the frosting. Add the sangria to a saucepan over moderate heat, bring to a boil then simmer for 10 minutes until the liquid is approximately a ¼ cup. Allow to completely cool.

6. Beat together the butter and salt, then beat in the powdered sugar a cup at a time until fluffy. Next, beat in the orange concentrate and syrupy sangria until incorporated and super fluffy.

7. Using a coring tool, make a well in the center of each cupcake and fill with the chilled filling. Next, frost with the buttercream. Enjoy!

About the Author

A native of Indianapolis, Indiana, Valeria Ray found her passion for cooking while she was studying English Literature at Oakland City University. She decided to try a cooking course with her friends and the experience changed her forever. She enrolled at the Art Institute of Indiana which offered extensive courses in the culinary Arts. Once Ray dipped her toe in the cooking world, she never looked back.

When Valeria graduated, she worked in French restaurants in the Indianapolis area until she became the head chef at one of the 5-star establishments in the area. Valeria's attention to taste and visual detail caught the eye of a local business person who expressed an interest in publishing her recipes. Valeria began her secondary career authoring cookbooks and e-books which she tackled with as much talent and gusto as her first career. Her passion for food leaps off the page of her books which have colourful anecdotes and stunning pictures of dishes she has prepared herself.

Valeria Ray lives in Indianapolis with her husband of 15 years, Tom, her daughter, Isobel and their loveable Golden Retriever, Goldy. Valeria enjoys cooking special dishes in her large, comfortable kitchen where the family gets involved in preparing meals. This successful, dynamic chef is an inspiration to culinary students and novice cooks everywhere.

Author's Afterthoughts

Thank you for Purchasing my book and taking the time to read it from front to back. I am always grateful when a reader chooses my work and I hope you enjoyed it!

With the vast selection available online, I am touched that you chose to be purchasing my work and take valuable time out of your life to read it. My hope is that you feel you made the right decision.

I very much would like to know what you thought of the book. Please take the time to write an honest and informative review on Amazon.com. Your experience and opinions will be of great benefit to me and those readers looking to make an informed choice.

With much thanks,

Valeria Ray

Printed in France by Amazon
Brétigny-sur-Orge, FR